T0042420

EVERYDAY SCIENCE

Science at the Grocery

Amy Sarver

PICTURE CREDITS
Cover background: Photodisc, Shopping List/Creatas; cover insets (middle left) Rubberball, Silhouettes of Occupations/Creatas, (bottom left), © Yoshio Tomii/SuperStock, (bottom right), © Myrleen Ferguson Cate/PhotoEdit; page 1 (top left), page 20 (top left) Rubberball, Silhouettes of Occupations/Creatas; page 1 (middle), page 12 (top left), page 20 (inset), page 21 (inset), page 23 (bottom middle), © David Young-Wolff/PhotoEdit; page 4 (top left) PhotoDisc, Eat, Drink, Dine/Creatas; pages 4-5 (bottom) Stone/Getty Images; page 5 (inset) StockImage/ImageState; page 6 (top left), © Yoshio Tomii/SuperStock; page 7 (all), pages 10-11 (bottom), © Jack Holtel/Photographik, Co.; page 8 (top left) PhotoDisc, Everyday Objects; page 8 (inset) Corbis, Business & Agriculture/Creatas; page 9 © Raoul Minsart/Masterfile; page 10 (top left) Stockbyte, Busy Kids 2/Creatas; page 11 (top right), page 16 (top left) The Mazer Corporation; page 12 (inset) Scimat/Photo Researchers; page 13 (inset) Imagesource, Kid's Health/Creatas; page 13 PhotoDisc/Getty Images; page 14 (top left), page 22 (bottom left), page 23 (bottom right bkgd), page 23 (top right) Food & Ingredients/Corbis Royalty FreeImages; page 14 (inset), © P. Parviainen/Photo Researchers; page 14-15 (bottom), © Neal Slavin/SuperStock; page 15 (inset), © Graham French/Masterfile; page 16 (inset) International Stock/ImageState, Inc.; page 17 © Jonathan A. Meyers/Stock Connection/PictureQuest; page 18 (top left) Stockbyte, Business Objects 2/Creatas; page 18 (inset) PhotoDisc, Shopping List/Creatas; pages 18-19 (bottom) Courtesy of NCR Corporation; page 21 Photodisc, Good Tastes/Creatas; page 23 (bottom middle) Groups-Children and Teenagers/Creatas

Produced through the worldwide resources of the National Geographic Society, John M. Fahey, Jr., President and Chief Executive Officer; Gilbert M. Grosvenor, Chairman of the Board; Nina D. Hoffman, Executive Vice President and President, Books and Education Publishing Group.

PREPARED BY NATIONAL GEOGRAPHIC SCHOOL PUBLISHING
Ericka Markman, Senior Vice President and President, Children's Books and Education Publishing Group; Steve Mico, Vice President, Editorial Director; Rosemary Baker, Executive Editor; Barbara Seeber, Editorial Manager; Jim Hiscott, Design Manager; Kristin Hanneman, Illustrations Manager; Matt Wascavage, Manager of Publishing Services; Sean Philpotts, Production Manager; Jane Ponton, Production Artist.

MANUFACTURING AND QUALITY MANAGEMENT: Christopher A. Liedel, Chief Financial Officer; Phillip L. Schlosser, Director; Clifton M.Brown, Maryclare Mcginty, Managers.

ART DIRECTION: Daniel Banks, Project Design Company

PROGRAM DEVELOPER: Kate Boehm Jerome

CONSULTANTS/REVIEWERS: Dr. Kathleen Marrs, Assistant Professor of Biology, Indiana University Purdue University Indianapolis; Dr. James Shymansky, E. Desmond Lee Professor of Science Education, University of Missouri-St. Louis.

BOOK DEVELOPMENT: The Mazer Corporation

Published by the National Geographic Society
Washington, D.C. 20036-4688

Product No. 4J41763

ISBN-13: 978-0-7922-4567-4
ISBN-10: 0-7922-4567-9

Printed in the United States of America

21 20 19 18
10 9 8 7 6 5

Contents

Going to the Grocery

Do you scream for ice cream? Can you eat a bowl of popcorn all by yourself? Whatever your favorite food may be, you can find it at the grocery store.

Thousands of items line the shelves. Shoppers zip through the aisles night and day. The grocery store hums with activity.

How does all that food stay fresh? How do you know where to find all the food you need? Science and technology have a lot to do with it. So grab a cart and let's explore the grocery store.

Check out the . . .

Doors That Open as You Enter

They pop wide open as you come near. They shut behind you after you walk through. What makes the doors at the grocery store move all by themselves?

Automatic doors may seem simple, but they are not. They are complex machines. They have many parts that work together to open and close the doors safely. Some use a **sensor** and motor system. The sensor above the door sends out a special light that can tell if something is near the door. When you walk toward the door, that something is you. The sensor sends out a signal that tells a motor to open the doors. A timer keeps the doors open long enough for you to walk into the store.

Suppose you stop to tie your shoelaces in the middle of the doorway. Lucky for you, most doors also have another set of sensors that keep you safe. These sensors are found along the inside edge of the doors. They will "see" you between the doors. Then the timer resets until you move through the doorway.

But there's even more to explore at the grocery store.

Check
out the . . .

Food, Food, and More Food

The shelves are tall. The aisles are long. How do people ever find what they want?

Similar foods are grouped together at the grocery store. That makes it easier to find things. Let's say you want to buy an apple. You know you can find apples with other fruits in the fruit section.

Grouping items is one way that grocery stores and scientists are alike. They both **classify** things.

When you classify something, you put it in a group with similar things. Just think about what you can find in the breakfast foods aisle. There are shelves full of cereal boxes. You can also find oatmeal and breakfast bars. Grocery stores classify these items so that you can easily find the foods you want.

But there's even more to explore at the grocery store.

Check out the . . .

Vegetable Showers

You lean over to look at the lettuce. The next thing you know, water is spraying on your head. What's happening?

Many grocery stores use misting to keep vegetables fresh. Misting is a process in which vegetables are sprayed with water. Pipes carry water to the section where vegetables are stored. Throughout the day, a light mist of water sprays over them. This helps to preserve the vegetables and to keep them firm and fresh.

The vegetables we eat are parts of plants. Plants have roots that take in water from the soil. When vegetables are taken out of the soil and sent to the grocery store, they no longer get water from the ground. Some vegetables, such as lettuce, can dry out. They need water to keep them crisp. That's why these vegetables get showers during the day.

But there's even more to explore at the grocery store.

Check out the . . .

Milk That Lasts

You pour it on your cereal at breakfast. You drink it again for dinner. How does milk stay fresh day after day?

Milk needs to be kept cold or else it will "go bad." Why does that happen? Milk sours because of a **chemical change**.

A chemical change happens when one substance changes into another substance. Food contains germs, called bacteria. When milk is left out, the germs in the milk cause the milk to spoil. The fresh milk changes into a new substance—sour milk. And once milk sours, you can't make it fresh again.

Bacteria like these turn milk sour.

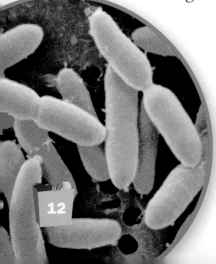

If you keep fresh milk in the refrigerator, though, it might last for a couple of weeks. How? In the 1800s, French scientist Louis Pasteur found a way to kill germs in food. He developed a process—later named for him—called **pasteurization**. In this process, food is heated at a high temperature for a period of time. The heat kills many of the germs that cause food to spoil. The milk you buy in the grocery is pasteurized. This means the milk is safe from harmful bacteria.

But there's even more to explore at the grocery store.

When milk spoils,
it tastes sour.

Check
out the . . .

Foods in the Freezer

You spot your favorite ice cream and open the glass door. A blast of cold air greets you. Why are some foods kept so cold?

Some food, like ice cream, is made to be eaten as a frozen treat. Other food, like pizza, is frozen so that it lasts longer without spoiling.

How do foods freeze? Most foods have water in them. Water freezes, or becomes a solid, when its temperature drops to 0°C (32°F). So freezers are set below this point. This keeps the food in a freezer frozen solid.

When water freezes, ice crystals form.

14

Suppose ice cream just sat on the shelf next to cans of corn. What would happen? You guessed it. The ice cream would melt into a runny ice cream soup.

When ice cream melts, a **physical change** happens. The ice cream doesn't change into another substance. It's still ice cream. But it changes from a frozen solid to a melted liquid. What if you stuck the melted ice cream back in the freezer? Another physical change would happen. It would change from a liquid back into a solid. Instead of sipping ice cream soup, you bite into frozen ice cream!

But there's even more to explore at the grocery store.

OPEN

Check out the . . .

Food Facts

Is it good for you? Or is it junk food? Read the label to find out!

Just about everything in the grocery has a label. Labels have loads of information. They tell you about the **nutrition** of the food. Nutrition is the science and study of food. If you look at a food label, you'll find a box called "Nutrition Facts." This box tells you what nutrients are in the food.

Most labels give the same kind of information. First, you can find out how many servings are in the container. You can also find out how many **calories** are in one serving. Calories are units for measuring the amount of energy in food. So the more calories a food has, the more energy you will get by eating the food.

You can also find out how much **fat, carbohydrate,** or **protein** is in foods. Your body needs just the right amounts of these nutrients. Labels also tell about some of the vitamins and minerals in foods. All of this information can help you and your family figure out what to eat.

But there's even more to explore at the grocery store.

Nutrition Facts
Serving Size 1 cup (252g)
Servings Per Container about 2

Amount Per Serving		% Daily Value*
Calories 470	Calories from Fat	
Total Fat 35g		53%
Saturated Fat 16g		81%
Cholesterol 90mg		30%
Sodium 1200mg		50%
Total Carbohydrate 25g		8%
Dietary Fiber 8g		35%
Sugars 1g		
Protein 21g		
Calcium 2%		Iron 10%

Nutrition Facts
Serving Size 2 bars (47g)
Servings Per Container 6

	2 bars	1 bar
	200	100
Calories		
Calories from Fat	60	30
	%DV*	%DV*
Total Fat 6g	9%	3g 5%
Saturated Fat 1g	4%	0g 0%
Cholesterol 0mg	0%	0mg 0%
Sodium 170mg	7%	85mg 4%
Total Carbohydrate 35g	12%	17g 6%
Dietary Fiber 3g	11%	1g 5%
Sugars 14g		7g
Protein 4g		2g
Iron	6%	
Thiamin		

Nutrition Facts
Serving Size 1 cup (29g)
Servings Per Container about 2

Amount Per Serving		% Daily Value*
Calories 110	Calories from Fat 10	
Total Fat 1g		2%
Saturated Fat 0g		0%
Saturated Fat 0.5g		
		0%
		30%
...ate 20g		7%
		14%

on Facts
...1/2 cup (55g)
...er Container about 7

	Cereal	Cereal with 1/2 cup Skim Milk
	210	250
...alories	20	20
	% Daily Value**	
Calories from Fat	3%	3%
Total Fat 2g*	3%	1%
Saturated Fat 0.5g	0%	5%
Cholesterol 0mg	0%	3%
Sodium 70mg	3%	17%
Total Carb. 44g	15%	11%
Dietary Fiber 3g	11%	
Sugars 17g		6%
Protein 4g		
Vitamin A	6%	8%
Vitamin C	6%	15%
Calcium	2%	10%
Iron	10%	10%

* Amount in Cereal. One half cup skim milk
contributes an additional 40 calories, 60mg
sodium, 6g total carbohydrates, and 4g protein.
** Percent Daily Values are based on a 2,000
calorie diet. Your daily values may be higher
or lower depending on your calorie needs.

	Calories	2,000	2,500
	Less than	65g	80g
	Less than	20g	25g
	Less than	300mg	300mg
	Less than	2,400mg	2,400mg
		300g	375g
		25g	30g

**Check
out the . . .**

Codes, Computers, and Costs

The clerk swipes the food over the scanner. The price pops up on the screen. How did the computer get so smart?

You've found the food you need. You head to the cashier and unload the cart. The cashier gets busy, passing each item over the **scanner.** In an instant, the item and its price appear on the cash register's display screen.

It takes a lot of technology to get you checked out at the grocery. Each item in the store has a bar code or a product number. These codes and numbers are entered into the store's computer system. Each code and number stands for an item. And each item gets a price. The small computers at the grocery are storehouses of huge amounts of information.

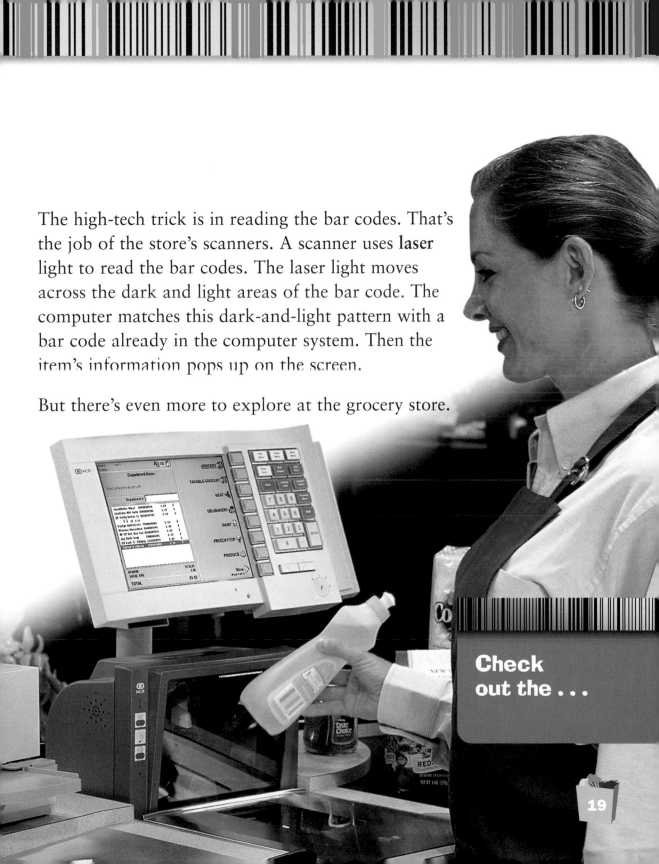

The high-tech trick is in reading the bar codes. That's the job of the store's scanners. A scanner uses **laser** light to read the bar codes. The laser light moves across the dark and light areas of the bar code. The computer matches this dark-and-light pattern with a bar code already in the computer system. Then the item's information pops up on the screen.

But there's even more to explore at the grocery store.

Check out the . . .

19

Paper or Plastic?

You might get this question when you check out. Which should you choose?

Grocery stores used to bag everything in brown paper bags. Then plastic bags came along. They are easy to make. They have built-in handles. And less energy is needed to make and deliver them to stores.

But for many people, paper is better than plastic. Why? All paper bags can be **recycled.** You can take them to a place where they are processed to make new products. Recycling paper prevents a lot of waste.

Reusable string bag

Plastic bags can also be recycled. But many recycling programs won't take plastic bags. That's because the process for recycling thin plastic bags is different from the process for recycling other plastic containers.

So which is better, paper or plastic? Some experts say neither. They say reusing bags is the answer. Save your bags after a trip to the grocery. Then use them again the next time you go shopping. You can also say "no thanks" when you don't need a bag.

Who would have thought that there was so much science to explore at the grocery store!

When you leave
the grocery,
you can . . .

Find Out More

Read On!

If you want to learn more about food and your body, check out these books.

Haduch, Bill. *Food Rules! The Stuff You Munch, Its Crunch, Its Punch, and Why You Sometimes Lose Your Lunch.* Puffin, 2001.

Rondeau, Amanda. *What Should I Eat?* Sandcastle, 2002.

Swanson, Diane. *Burp! The Most Interesting Book You'll Ever Read About Eating.* Kids Can Press, 2001.

Log On!

Check out *www.fightbac.org* to learn about how to fight the germs in food. This USDA website shows you how to fight BAC—that is, how to keep food safe from bacteria, the tiny germs that can spoil food.

Go to this Team Nutrition website for news about nutrition. Just type in *www.fns.usda.gov/tn/Students/Fun/index.html* and you can play games, click on food-filled links, and learn how food keeps you healthy.

Imagine That!

Imagine that you are the manager of a brand new grocery store. Your store has five aisles with shelves on each side. The store also has one row of freezers and a refrigerated section. Use graph paper to draw a diagram that shows the aisles, the freezers, and each area of the store. Label the foods stored in each area. Share your picture with the class and tell why you chose to store certain foods in each area.

Glossary

calorie—a unit for measuring the amount of energy in food

carbohydrate—a nutrient that can be used when your body needs quick energy

chemical change—a process in which one substance changes into another substance

classify—to group things based on how they are alike

fat—a nutrient that can be stored under your skin as a supply of energy

laser—a high-energy beam of light

nutrition—the science of food; the study of how nutrients affect human health

pasteurization—a method of killing some harmful germs in milk and other foods by heating them to a high temperature for a period of time

physical change—a process in which a substance changes in form but does not become a new substance

protein—a nutrient that helps build and repair parts of your body

recycle—to make waste materials, such as paper or glass, into new materials

scanner—a device that uses a laser to read bar codes

sensor—a device that reacts to heat or light